WHO MADE MY LUNCH?

FROM MILK TO ICE CREAM

BY BRIDGET HEOS · ILLUSTRATED BY STEPHANIE FIZER COLEMAN

AMICUS ILLUSTRATED and **AMICUS INK**
are published by Amicus
P.O. Box 227, Mankato, MN 56002
www.amicuspublishing.us

LIBRARY OF CONGRESS
CATALOGING-IN-PUBLICATION DATA
Names: Heos, Bridget, author. | Coleman, Stephanie Fizer, illustrator. | Heos, Bridget. Who made my lunch?
Title: From milk to ice cream / by Bridget Heos ; illustrated by Stephanie Fizer Coleman.
Description: Mankato, MN : Amicus, [2018] | Series: Who made my lunch?
Identifiers: LCCN 2016057204 (print) | LCCN 2017000277 (ebook) | ISBN 9781681511214 (library binding) | ISBN 9781681512112 (ebook) | ISBN 9781681521466 (pbk.)
Subjects: LCSH: Ice cream, ices, etc.—Juvenile literature. | Dairy products—Juvenile literature.
Classification: LCC TX795 .H54 2018 (print) | LCC TX795 (ebook) | DDC 641.86/2—dc23
LC record available at https://lccn.loc.gov/2016057204

EDITOR: Rebecca Glaser
DESIGNER: Kathleen Petelinsek

ABOUT THE AUTHOR
Bridget Heos is the author of more than 80 books for children. She lives in Kansas City with her husband and four children. Her favorite ice cream is pralines and cream.

ABOUT THE ILLUSTRATOR
Stephanie Fizer Coleman is an illustrator, tea drinker, and picky eater from West Virginia, where she lives with her husband and two silly dogs. When she's not drawing, she's getting her hands dirty in the garden or making messes in the kitchen.

An ice cream treat is as easy as one, two, three scoops!

But what if you had to make the ice cream yourself?

And also milk the cows and grow the sugar?

Grab your sunscreen! You're now a dairy farmer in sunny California. And you need to raise some cows. When cows give birth to calves, the mothers produce milk.

Machines milk the cows. Then a tanker truck takes the milk to a creamery.

At the creamery, the milk is separated. A big machine spins the milk. The cream goes into one tank. The milk goes into the other.

Both the skim milk and the cream are put in
tanker trucks. Next stop, the ice cream factory!

But wait. You want sweet ice cream, right? You'll need sugar. You can grow sugarcane in sunny Florida. Start by planting pieces of sugarcane.

The sugarcane pieces will grow into new plants.
Sugarcane is thirsty! Water it well. It can take
up to two years to grow.

At harvest time, cut down the plants with a cane harvester.
This machine also chops the sugarcane into smaller pieces.
Now hurry! Get the sugarcane to the mill before it dries out.

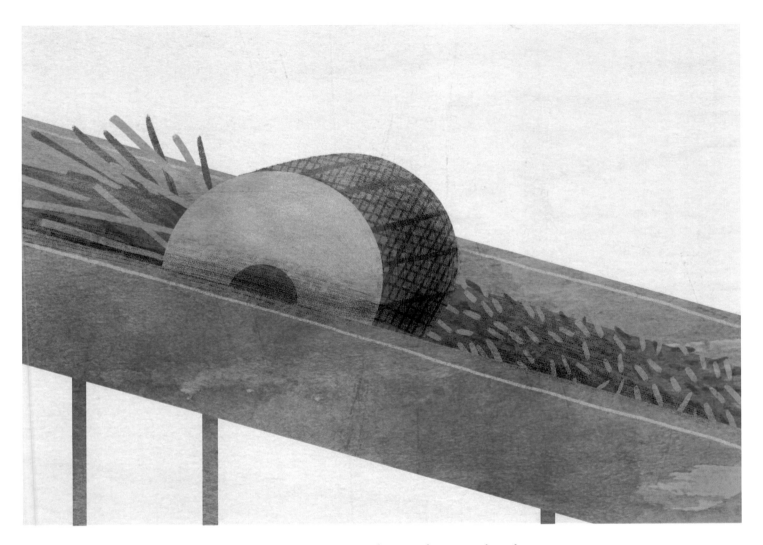

Just in time! At the mill, shred and crush the sugarcane. Collect the juice and boil it. Add sugar crystals, which help new crystals grow. Then send this raw sugar to a refinery.

At the refinery, the sugar is boiled and allowed to crystalize again. These new crystals make up the sugar we eat. Sweet! Now you have all the main ingredients for ice cream.

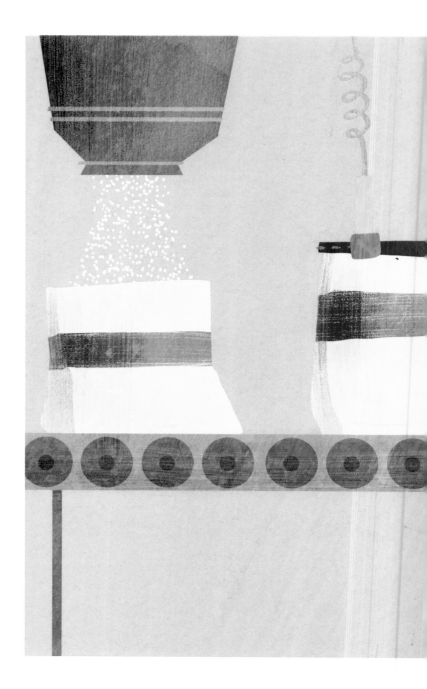

Let's make some ice cream! At the factory, milk and cream are pumped through tubes into a mixing tank. Add some of that delicious sugar! For chocolate ice cream, add cocoa, too.

Now pasteurize, or heat, the mixture. This kills bad bacteria. Pump the hot mixture into the homogenizer. This breaks the fat into tiny particles, which makes the ice cream smoother.

Send the mixture into a freezer room, where it is cooled in tanks. From here, pump it over to the flavor vats. Now, you can add liquid flavors, such as mint, vanilla, or fruit juice.

The mixture may be cold, but it's still not ice cream. This machine makes the magic happen! When the mixture touches the cold sides, it freezes. Rotating blades scrape it off the sides.

Now the ice cream is squirted into containers. The ice cream is frozen, but still soft. To harden, it travels on a conveyor belt through a room that's 30°F (34°C) **below** zero. Brrr!

A freezer truck carries the ice
cream to the grocery store.

Thanks to the dairy farmers, sugarcane farmers, and ice cream factory workers, you have a delicious treat to eat!

WHERE ARE DAIRY COWS AND SUGARCANE FOUND?

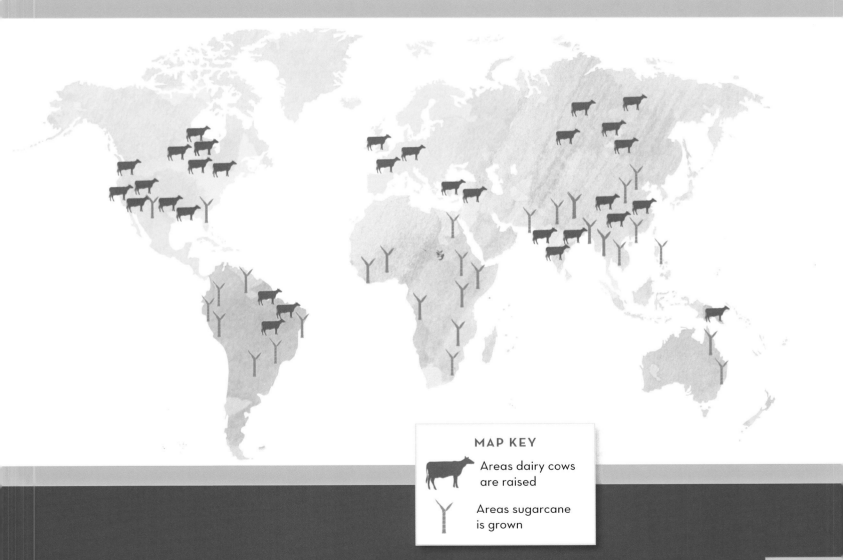

MAP KEY

Areas dairy cows are raised

Areas sugarcane is grown

GLOSSARY

bacteria Microscopic, single-celled living things that can be either helpful or harmful.

cream The fatty liquid that rises to the top of milk.

homogenizer A machine that uses high pressure to break fat particles into smaller pieces.

pasteurize To heat to a high temperature for the purpose of killing harmful bacteria.

raw sugar Sugar that still has some of the juices present in sugarcane.

refinery A factory where juices and impurities are removed from sugar.

READ MORE

Bailey, R. J. *Ice Cream: How Is It Made?* Minneapolis: Jump!, Inc., 2016.

Herrington, Lisa M. *Milk to Ice Cream.* New York: Children's Press, 2013.

Williams, Bonnie. *The Scoop on Ice Cream.* New York: Simon Spotlight, 2014.

WEBSITES

Discover Dairy
http://www.discoverdairy.com/
Watch a video and find other resources about milk production.

How We Make Ice Cream
http://www.benjerry.com/flavors/ how-we-make-ice-cream
Read about the steps used in making ice cream and watch ice cream factory workers tell about their jobs.

Sugarcane: Paddock to Plate
https://www.youtube.com/ watch?v=tyNDJHkLyrE
A young girl and a farmer from Australia explain how sugarcane is grown, harvested, and processed into sugar.

Every effort has been made to ensure that these websites are appropriate for children. However, because of the nature of the Internet, it is impossible to guarantee that these sites will remain active indefinitely or that their contents will not be altered.